How Long or How Wide?

A Measuring Guide

To Renee
—B.P.C.

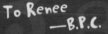

Length:
The distance
from one end
of something
to the other

A short note about length:
People in the United States and Canada have two systems to measure length.
One is called the English system, or the U.S. customary system. It uses inches,
feet, and yards. The other system is called the metric system, or International
System of Units. It uses millimeters, centimeters, decimeters, and meters. People
in many countries use only the metric system.

How Long or How Wide?

A Measuring Guide

by Brian P. Cleary

illustrated by Brian Gable

M MILLBROOK PRESS / MINNEAPOLIS

A table,
a teacher,
a building,
or creature,
a stuffed teddy bear
that you've treasured,

LENGTH

What size are they all?
The big and the small?
Each one of these things
can be measured!

Length answers the riddle
for large things or little.

How l o n g
or how tall
or how wide
is that
swing?

or your ring?

Or a dinosaur wing?

or the ladder that leads to the slide?

INCH

1 inch looks like this, and it's easy to miss, because of its very small size.

But it shows us its might
when it helps tell the height
of the trees that reach up to the skies.

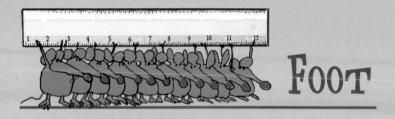

FOOT

12 inches together
make 1 foot, so whether
you measure a desk or a door,

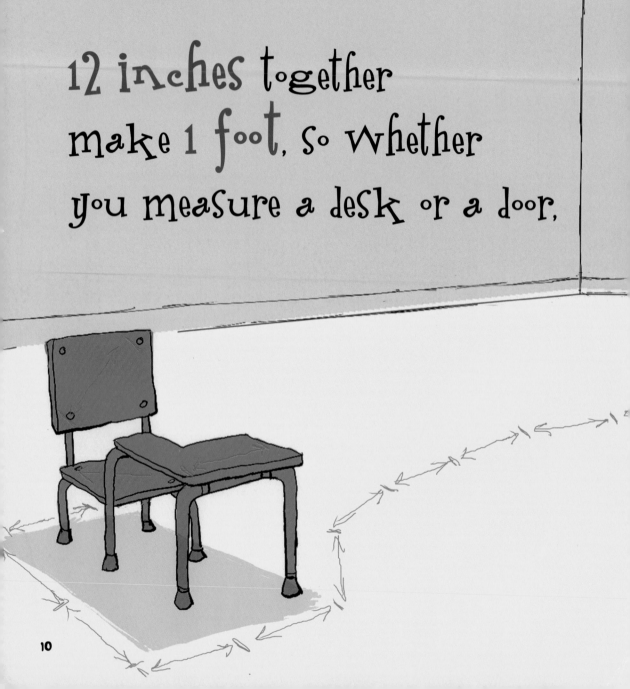

each 12-inch-long line
is a definite sign
that you've measured another foot more.

And see this—it's cool—
inches live on this tool.

It's a measuring stick
called a ruler.

A 12-inch collection,
1 foot of perfection,

the right size
for every grade-schooler!

Now, 3 of these feet,
should they line up
and meet,

1 Yard →

← 3 Feet

together are what's called 1 yard.

14

That's **36** inches,
and here's what the cinch is:
that's also **3** feet—it's not hard!

If you measured your bed
and the yardstick had said
that your headboard's exactly 3 feet,

16

You could say that the height
is 1 yard,
and you're right—
or 36 inches—
how neat!

It's really quite wise
When you're measuring size
to know more than
only one system.

E

ENGLISH

The terms here are fun,

METRIC

and before we are done,
you'll surely be able to list 'em!

MILLIMETER

It's nearly as thin
as a needle or pin.
1 inch holds almost 26.

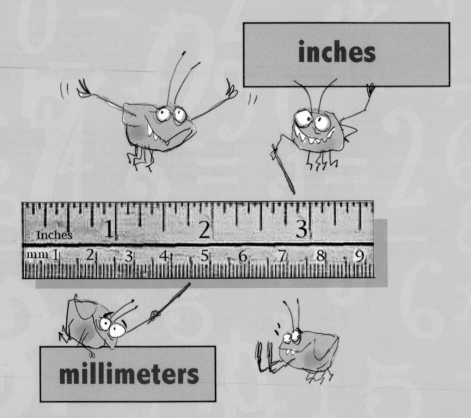

inches

millimeters

Put your face really near,
that's the whole thing right here.

Inches 1
mm 1 2

It's smaller
than most fleas and ticks!

CENTIMETER

Take your fingers and pinch less than half of 1 inch.

A dime would quite easily hide one.

1 centimeter

As small as it is,
when you're asked on a quiz,
there are 10 millimeters
inside 1!

DECIMETER

A bit less than 4 inches,
really no more.
   There are 10 centimeters
tucked in it.

1
2
3
4
5
6
7
8
9
10

DECIMETER

DECIMETER

100 would be
the amount you would see
of all millimeters within it.

METER

| 1 meter |
| 1 yard |

Just how tall is Peter?

He's all of 1 meter.

It's a little bit more than 1 yard.

Or you could say Peter's just 10 decimeters,

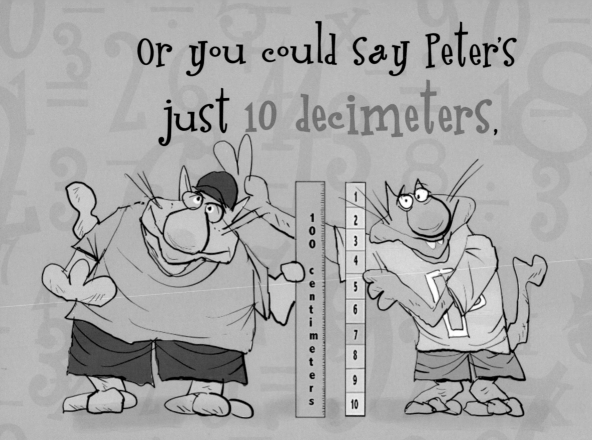

and watch as your paper is starred!

Now it's a pleasure
because you can measure,

which makes you the ultimate ruler!

So, what is length?

Do you know?

English Length Measurements

1 yard = 3 feet = 36 inches
1 foot = 12 inches

Metric Length Measurements

1 meter = 10 decimeters
= 100 centimeters = 1,000 millimeters

1 centimeter = 10 millimeters

1 yard ↘

↖ 3 feet

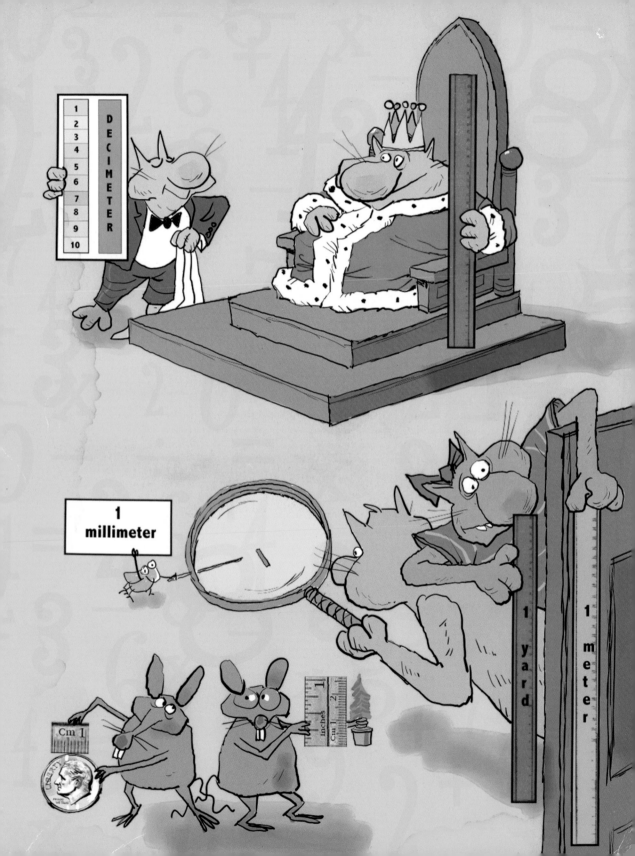

ABOUT THE AUTHOR & ILLUSTRATOR

BRIAN P. CLEARY is the author of the Words Are CATegorical©, Math Is CATegorical©, Adventures in Memory™, and Sounds Like Reading™ series. He has also written The Laugh Stand: Adventures in Humor, Peanut Butter and Jellyfishes: A Very Silly Alphabet Book, and two poetry books. Mr. Cleary lives in Cleveland, Ohio.

BRIAN GABLE is the illustrator of several Words Are CATegorical© books, as well as the Math Is CATegorical© series. Mr. Gable also works as a political cartoonist for the Globe and Mail newspaper in Toronto, Canada.

Text copyright © 2007 by Brian P. Cleary
Illustrations copyright © 2007 by Lerner Publishing Group, Inc.

Millbrook Press
A division of Lerner Publishing Group, Inc.
241 First Avenue North
Minneapolis, MN 55401 U.S.A.

Website address: www.lernerbooks.com

Library of Congress Cataloging-in-Publication Data

Cleary, Brian P., 1959-
    How long or how wide? : a measuring guide / Brian P. Cleary ; illustrated by
Brian Gable.
       p.   cm. — (Math is categorical)
    ISBN 978-0—8225—6694—6 (lib. bdg. : alk. paper)
    ISBN 978-1—58013—646—4 (eBook)
    1. Length measurement—Juvenile literature. I. Title. II. Series: Cleary,
Brian P., 1959- Math is categorical.
    QC102.C58 2007
    530.8—dc22   2006010754

Manufactured in the United States of America
6 — BP — 6/1/13